10,⁰⁰

In The Spirit of Adventure
A 1915 Mount Mitchell Hiking Journal
Written by D. R. Beeson

IN THE SPIRIT OF ADVENTURE

A 1915 Mount Mitchell Hiking Journal
May 21-24, 1915

By

D. R. Beeson, Sr.

With A Story By His Hiking Partner,
C. Hodge Mathes

Edited By
Norma Myers
Ned Irwin
Charles W. Maynard

Panther Press SEYMOUR TENNESSEE

ISBN   1-887205-00-4 Paperback
ISBN   1-887205-01-2 Hardback

Panther Press
P.O. Box 636
Seymour, Tennessee 37865
423-579-5792

Book Design by Robyn R. Sauve of Rusk Design, 401 Rainey Road, Starr, SC 29684
Cover Design by David Morris of Panther Press and Robyn R. Sauve.

This Work Is Dedicated To
D. R. Beeson, Sr.
And His Friend,
C. Hodge Mathes
Who Roamed the Mountains
In the Spirit of Adventure

The writer's royalty is being given to the Archives of Appalachia at East Tennessee State University in Johnson City, Tennessee.

The Archives of Appalachia serve the region by preserving and providing access to records of historical and research value pertaining to the political, social, economic, and cultural development of the Southern Mountains. The original journal with other Beeson materials is in The Archives of Appalachia.

For more information write:
Archives of Appalachia
Archives and Special Collections Of the Sherrod Library
East Tennessee State University
Box 70665
Johnson City, Tennessee 37614-0665

INTRODUCTION

Mount Mitchell is the eastern United States' premier peak at 6,684 feet above sea level. For that reason Mt. Mitchell beckoned to D.R. (Don) Beeson and C. Hodge Mathes as a place for yet another hiking adventure. The two friends set off in May of 1915 on what would be the last great adventure that Beeson documented with a photographic journal. The two had already walked to Roan and Grandfather Mountains in 1913, to Table Rock Mountain in the spring of 1914, and across the crest line of the Great Smoky Mountains in the late summer of 1914.

The driving force for the two friends appears to have been a need to see virtually unknown territory. Beeson reveled in the conquest of this highest of eastern peaks, so much so, that he climbed a tree when he reached the summit in order to write in his journal that this was the highest he had ever been. A wonderful display of excitement and playfulness!

Vast changes separate me from Beeson's and Mathes' world of eighty years ago. The Blue Ridge Parkway delivers me to the base of the mighty mountain, while a road winds to the top. A tower permits a clearer and higher view than did Beeson's tree, but, that view isn't as clear as it once was. The spruce-fir forest which covers the mountaintop is laboring under attack from the balsam wooly adelgid and air pollution. People crowd the summit on warm, clear days to catch a glimpse of what Beeson and Mathes toiled hard days and hours to obtain.

I'm struck by the closeness of Beeson and Mathes to the history of the area. They went to Mt. Mitchell fifty-seven years after the Rev. Elisha Mitchell fell to his death trying to prove his claim of the peak's highest status. They were guided on their trip by Dolph Wilson, the son of Mitchell's guide, Big Tom Wilson. Big Tom himself had died just a few years before Beeson and Mathes went.

The monument which marked Mitchell's grave had been wrecked only a few months when the two arrived. The entire mountain would be protected by the state of North Carolina as a state park the very next year in 1916. History was still much at hand when the two adventured. They thrilled in hearing about the escapades of their predecessors. The accounts in this volume display how the two reacted to all that they experienced.

The story of Rev. Elisha Mitchell and General Thomas Clingman is best left for Beeson and Mathes to tell. As is their own adventure. This volume closes the *In The Spirit of Adventure* series but it was not the last adventure for the two men. They remained friends and hiking partners for many years, but their long adventures came to an end on this trek. Much changed in the years from 1913 to 1915. Mathes' children were getting older. Beeson was to be married. The world was becoming involved in a war in Europe which caused a demand for timber from the eastern mountains and a restriction of other resources. Beeson and Mathes made other hikes and walks of shorter duration together. They both remained interested in and advocates for the beautiful mountain region which they had explored.

It is my hope that this book and the other three in the series will perpetuate the grand spirit in which these two men ranged the mountains. Their hikes are fascinating windows onto a moment in the history of the area. Their words and photographs provide valuable materials for the study of the Appalachian Mountains as an ecosystem and as a culture.

The four journals stand as monuments to the two men, D. R. (Don) Beeson and C. Hodge Mathes, who went into the wild southern mountains In The Spirit of Adventure.

Charles W. Maynard
Executive Director
Friends of Great Smoky Mountains National Park
1995

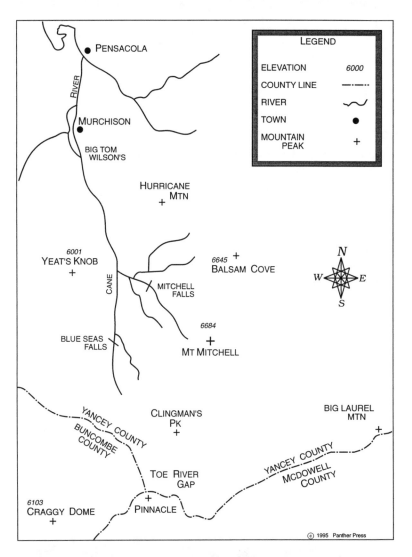

Points of interest which Beeson and Mathes mention. A map of their exact route has not been found.

A NOTE ABOUT THE JOURNAL

The original journal which D. R. Beeson prepared is now in The Archives of Appalachia at East Tennessee State University in Johnson City, Tennessee. Many of D. R. Beeson's papers, journals, maps and photographs are held by The Archives of Appalachia.

Mr. Beeson actually kept a handwritten journal on the trail. When he returned from the hike, he had his handwritten field notes typed into a booklet which he illustrated with his photographs. The Mt. Mitchell hike was the last of four adventures with C. Hodge Mathes. It appears that this journal was put together years after the hike. Beeson mentions that part of his notes were lost. He also includes pictures of Mrs. Beeson at the summit of Mt. Mitchell many years after the hike.

This edition of Beeson's hike journal from 1915 attempts to preserve the look of the original. The text, photographs and captions are as Beeson wrote and arranged them. Only minor editing was done in order to make the text clearer and read more smoothly. The photographs were prepared from original photographs because the negatives were not available. No map showing the route was prepared by Beeson. The map included locates the points of interest mentioned in the text.

C. Hodge Mathes' story "A Saga of the Carolina Hills" was published in The High Road in 1929. It is included because it is Mathes' representation, in narrative form, of the information and experiences from the 1915 hike.

The following is a representation of the original journal but not a facsimile. The editors and publisher attempted to preserve the character of the original while presenting an attractive book which can be kept and treasured as the actual journal is.

A WALKING AND CAMPING TRIP
TO
MOUNT MITCHELL, NORTH CAROLINA

Here we are at Dolph Wilson's Hotel and just started on another mountain trip consisting of the same old pair, C. Hodge Mathes and D. R. Beeson, the writer of this narrative.

We left Johnson City on the C.C. & O. at Eleven this morning with the idea of another good trip after having done Grandfather, Table Rock and the Smokies on three previous and very tough and enjoyable excursions. Our packs are the lightest yet and will run to about twenty-five pounds for each of us. I'm carrying four dozen double-coated plates for my camera which has three interchangeable lenses plus filters and duplicator; it looks most any dub could get good pictures with such an outfit.

Each time we go we take less beans and more milk chocolate and this will probably [be] the last trip we take where Boston will have any voice in the proceedings at all. Meat, biscuits, coffee and chocolate is about all that's needed. Two years ago when we took the first of these trips we thought we couldn't get enough beans but I guess we made a mistake. On this trip we don't propose to cook or even heat up anything but our coffee. Our little old sleeping tent has been packed wet so much that it isn't quite as waterproof as it used to be,- except on moonlight nights. We have the best packs yet,-a wide strap over each shoulder and made of waterproof stuff. Then, of course, we have our usual rattlesnake "nannygoat", the hypodermic variety. Also of course, thermos bottles, pneumatic mattresses, dress suits, etc. They say these Black Mountain Bears are mighty particular about the social conventions.

Our host tonight, Dolph Wilson, killed his 100th bear this past winter but he traps the poor things and then shoots them without giving them any show at all. He is a famous hunter in these parts,-a small man, bald and apparently quiet but not absolutely. He was born in 1861 in a log cabin near here and has lived pretty close home all his life. His father was Big Tom Wilson, probably the most famous native of this section and one of the few I ever heard of that was not a grandson of Daniel Boone. Big Tom's cabin is just up the valley.

We got here at 6 P.M. Eastern Time so had time to take a half dozen pictures with good light before supper,-a couple of the valley and Big Tom's cabin and his later cabin where my companion posed on the front porch beside a beautiful descendent of Big Tom's (feminine) called Niagara Falls Riddle. She was considerably concerned about educational matters and, of course, the Deacon couldn't be so impolite as to withhold anything he knew on the subject. The picture was a half-second exposure but we took up three quarters of an

C. Hodge Mathes and Niagara Falls Riddle, Big Tom Wilson's grandaughter.

hour including the educational quiz. However, if Niagara falls for the educational dope, the Normal School, where the Deacon presides, will get an increased enrollment,-so I guess the time was well spent.

Supper was good and presided over by two visiting preachers. We have engaged Dolph to guide us to the top,-much against his wishes,-past the small water fall where Dr. Mitchell lost his life. He says there is no trail to the spot and we can't make it in one day,-we have persuaded him to risk it.

As usual, the Deacon found about 146 mutual acquaintances with Dolph. He has the blamedest memory for people and their names I ever saw.

Toe River Gap
8:15 P.M., Saturday Night,
May 22, 1915

After a good sleep at Dolph's we got breakfast at 6:30 and started out for the heights a little after seven thirty. Before leaving we took a picture of Dolph standing beside the hide of his 100th. bear; also we read the account in an Asheville newspaper, written by Big Tom himself, of his finding of Dr. Mitchell's body.

We started out up the valley some two miles, turning into the mountains at Brown Bros. lumber camp. We passed Big Tom's cabin again and the Doc kept his hat and tie on till we got past where Niagara can be seen from; he's a man that sure is fond of scenery but Niagara was soon lost to view.

Well, we reached the Mitchell Falls about eleven, Dolph smelling out the trail like a hound and hitting the stream not a hundred feet above the falls, and

he said he hadn't been there for nine years. Scarcely any sight-seers ever come this way,-approximately none, in fact. The Mitchell Falls is on a small mountain stream that heads on the west slope of Mt. Mitchell itself and flows into the Caney River. The height of the fall is not over twenty feet and the stream is nothing but a brook and a pool about fifteen feet deep has been worn in the rock below and is probably fifteen feet in diameter. We sat beside the pool and listened to Dolph tell the story of the explorer of the highest peak east of the Mississippi and his death in the pool at our feet and of the hunt for his body. It seems that the Rev. Elisha Mitchell, D.D. was a professor of math in the University of North Carolina and had visited the Black Mountain Country in 1846 and had Wm. Wilson, a cousin of Big Tom, to guide him to Yeates Knob, across the Caney valley from the high peaks of the Blacks, from which point he took observations with a pocket instrument of some sort and declared that the peak now bearing his name is the highest of the range and of the whole eastern

part of country. However, the honor of having first measured the height of the peak was claimed by Hon. T. L. Clingman, a North Carolina Congressman and the matter was even discussed in the U. S. Congress we were told, where it was decided in favor of Clingman. Mitchell, however, decided to measure the altitude of the peak accurately and, in the spring of 1857, came to Asheville and started from a bench mark there, to run a line of levels to the top. It was slow work, of course, and was not finished for the last seen of him alive was when he left his camp near the top on the evening of June 27, bound for the settlement on Caney. Nothing having been heard of him for several days, search was started on the fifth day after his disappearance but without result for some four days.

It was then that the news was brought to Big Tom Wilson. He at once supposed that Dr. Mitchell had in all probability taken the trail he had followed going to the top on his first visit, and so, on reaching the top next day he laid

his course accordingly. Before he had gone far he saw tracks in the soft earth and from there on had little difficulty. Following the trail further Big Tom announced where darkness had overtaken Dr. Mitchell, because he was kicking the rocks and logs instead of stepping over them as before. The party camped well down the slope and before going far next morning,-the morning of the eleventh day after the disappearance,-they came to the falls we were then sitting beside and found the body in this pool; he had evidently had trouble getting along in the dark for in daylight a man could not possibly have lost his footing where Dolph showed us, and slid down the moderately steep earth bank that lies between there and the edge of the cliff that drops straight down into the pool. The vertical drop looks like about fifteen feet at that point, not enough to be specially dangerous unless, as Dolph says his Father always thought, he struck his head against a big balsam log lying across the pool. And, as I've said before, the pool is only a few feet across and ought to be easy to get out of,

even in the dark. The body was taken to Asheville and buried there on the 10th of July but was moved, at the request of his friends, in the summer of 1858 and placed on the summit of the peak that bears his name. A monument of case bronze was erected over the grave but was so shot to pieces and hacked up by curio hunters that all but the base was blown over in a severe storm a few months ago. They say it will be replaced. We got a couple of pictures of Mitchell's Pool with Dolph pointing to the spot where the body was found, but I'm a little afraid I did not give them a long enough exposure.

Well, after leaving the falls, we struck up a little ravine with about the same slope as a telegraph pole and, about noon, found a flat place big enough to eat dinner off of.   Dolph acted sort of clannish and refused to eat any of our grub at all except one small biscuit; he sat on a log and ate what he had brought with him and was medium quiet for the first time since we started. I've seen men before who could walk up a steep mountain as fast as he can but have never

known one before who could talk incessantly while doing it. I don't believe he knows what it is to get out of breath.

About half an hour after dinner we ran into a storm and stopped under a cliff for a while. It didn't rain long but the undergrowth had been breaking our own course and not following any trail. About this time we travelled for about half an hour in the worst going I ever got through alive. In lots of places there was not even room to crawl flat on the ground without removing our packs and shoving them before us. It was most all laurel and I guess Dolph didn't know it was sacred to Apollo for he cussed it out most unsacredly. It was about a half mile and set a slow speed record. We came to standing room occasionally and the views of the mountains were great.

We made the top about half past two and Dolph said we were the best walkers he had ever seen; he was a lot relieved as he had been worrying a

good deal about not getting out of the mountains before dark; seemed to dread the snakes more than anything else.

We saw lots of bear and deer tracks and places where bears had torn the bark off trees. I tried chewing a piece of balsam gum but don't like it. It gets pink when you chew it and gives an inside taste like a couple of coats of white lead and linseed oil.

The top of Mitchell,-elevation 6711,-was covered with clouds which prevented our seeing anything so we went down to the mountain house and sat for half an hour. It's a sort of a summer hotel combined with a government weather station,-formerly had wireless but this had been discontinued. There was a bad looking gang in charge and one of them named Bill had just come from serving Uncle Sam in Mexico. He had just set up a small gasoline engine and dynamo and had put the electric lights in service today for the first time.

Mountain House, Mt. Mitchell - 1914.

We left with Dolph about 3:30 and went back up to the peak about a hundred yards away but had no more luck than before as the clouds were still there, so we started for the Pinnacle and Toe River Gap. A short distance from the top we came to a cleared half acre where several trails came in and where Dr. Mitchell turned to the right to go to his death. Dolph took the beaten track toward home and we took to the left down a lumber skidway to the Pearley & Crockett Lumber Co. logging railway, a narrow gauge Shay geared affair that runs from a few hundred feet of the top of Mt. Mitchell, twenty miles south down to Beech Mountain Station on the Southern Railway.

We soon got down below the clouds and found the air fairly clear and getting better but by no means perfect. Table Rock and the Hawksbill were in plain sight some fifteen miles to the east and Grandfather more to the north and about 40 miles off. The mountains are fine to look at but not so impressive as the endless big ridges of the Great Smokies.

South from Mt. Mitchell - 1914.

We have a mighty pretty camp and a good though backward fire. Everything up here seems to be soaked through making poor facilities for building campfires. We are about five miles from Mt. Mitchell and on a bank close by the railroad where we have watched several log trains pass and one motorcycle. The whole mountain from here to the top on the east side is bare and burned over and not a pleasant sight at all.

Elevation 6725
2 P.M. Sunday May 23

This location is too precarious for an extended entry so will close and come down.

(Made in the top of a balsam tree on top of Mt. Mitchell. This is the highest I have ever been above sea level).

Blue Sea Falls
8 P.M. Sunday, May 23

This is, without doubt, the most beautiful spot I have ever camped in. This Blue Sea Fork of the Caney is a good sized stream and drops over a cliff about sixty feet high into a round pool a hundred feet across and goodness knows how deep.

This pool is quite a place; the sides rise so steeply from the water that it's dangerous to explore except at the right side where we are camped, where there is a shelf of rock with dirt veneer that just gives room for the tent and fire. It's about ten feet above the water and straight up.

We left camp at the Toe River Gap at 7:30 this morning after a good light and a light breakfast. The weather all day has been fairly poor for long distance work with the camera but the cloud effects were wonderful.

The Pinnacle of the Blue Ridge,-the highest point on the whole length of the Ridge,-is a little over 5600 feet in elevation and was just above our camp to the south, and we hiked to the top in half an hour. It's a bare grassy knob and gives all the views you can wish and in all directions. The hogs worried us some in getting our pictures and the Deacon got so immersed in the scenery that he failed to assist in keeping the animals away from the camera. So I spoiled three plates and got just a little out of humor. But it's in occasions like that that the Doc shows his class for he never gets ruffled at all no matter what happens; I can act like a pup and he never gets a bit dogmatic.

We got back to last night's camp at 9:30, packed up and started back for Mitchell along the logging road and certainly enjoyed the walk and the constant gamble of getting rain soaked. But we were lucky and only got wet once,-about the middle of the afternoon.

Pinnacle, highest point on Blue Ridge - 1915.

We made the high peak by noon and ate lunch (dinner) on the very top, close to Dr. Mitchell's grave and what's left of the monument. The clouds held off for a while and we saw the country very well, the Great Craggy Mountains to the west, over 6100 feet above sea level being the most imposing. It was all about what we had expected it to be.

After eating we went down the mountain to the Mountain House to say goodbye to the folks and ran across a couple of very nice chaps from Asheville who had come up for the day. The weather was looking bad again, though, so we didn't tarry long but made a start for the lower regions.

And by the way, there's a murderer with a price on his head, supposed to be hiding hereabouts but we're not looking for the reward.

We made it down to Brown Bros. in two hours and forty minutes, taking some pictures en route and rubbering at the scenery frequently. Not far from

the bottom of the trail we passed the famous big poplar tree, the biggest tree I have ever seen and is said to be eleven feet thick at the butt,-it looked it.

From Brown Bros. to the Blue Sea Falls is about three miles and it took us a little over an hour.

N. B. The diary from here is lost but the trip was about over and we had only to go back by Dolph Wilson's and down to the C.C.& O. at Pensacola (I Believe). At any rate this day, May 24, was set forth on the first page of the diary as the end of the trip, so I can't see that much was lost when the rest of the story was lost.

- FINIS -

Donald Richard Beeson, Sr.
(1881-1983)

In the spirit of adventure, D.R. (Donald Richard) Beeson, Sr. moved to West Virginia to explore what to him was described as a yet untamed frontier. Beeson joined a tide of professionals who migrated to the Appalachians around the turn of the century as a part of the increasing industrial development of the region. His work with United States Steel in the coal fields and with the Clinchfield Railroad certainly would be worthy of study within the context of the economic history of southern Appalachia, but it is his love of the outdoors that makes his story special.

Beeson was born in 1881 in Uniontown, Pennsylvania. He was the youngest of three children in one of the leading families of Uniontown. His father, William Beeson, educated at Yale and Harvard, was an attorney and businessman. When D.R. Beeson, Sr. was seven, his mother Mary Conn Beeson died of tuberculosis. His mother's sister, Rebecca Conn, took over the responsibility for his care. The family maintained a residence in Uniontown so the children could attend school there, but Beeson spent his early years at Mount Braddock, a 1,500 acre family estate located six miles from Uniontown. Beeson remembered his childhood at Mount Braddock as a happy time, in summer hiking into the mountains to camp or swim, and in winter skating on the ponds or "coasting down the hills." In a reminiscence of his early life, Beeson recalled that he "ran wild" over the estate and "knew every stream and woods."[1]

In 1888, his father's business failed, and in the economic depression of the 1890s, the family's wealth was lost. The family sold the Mount Braddock estate in 1891 and lived in Uniontown the year round. At age 10, Beeson began working as a newspaper boy where, as he described it, he learned the "survival of the fittest." After graduating from high school, he worked pitching hay on a farm. Beeson left Uniontown in 1898 to live with his aunt, Louisa Hamilton, in Washington, Pennsylvania. He attended Washington and Jefferson College, where he studied mathematics. Lacking the funds to continue his education, Beeson was forced to quit college at the end of his sophomore year.[2]

In 1900, Beeson began working for the H.C. Frick Coal and Coke Company in western Pennsylvania. He earned thirty-five dollars the first month as a chainman for an underground engineering force in the coal mines near Connellsville. Within the next year, he moved to Scottdale to work as a draftsman in the company's main office. With the organization of U.S. Steel, the drafting department of H.C. Frick Coal and Coke Company was moved to Ambridge, Pennsylvania. By 1902, Beeson was working as a draftsman for the American Bridge Company, a subsidiary of U.S. Steel, which handled the steel construction operations for the new corporation.

In the spring of 1902, Beeson moved to Gary, West Virginia, as a part of the corporation's efforts to start a new coal operation on lands purchased in McDowell County. Beeson later related that "[m]ost all the boys in the Ambridge office wanted to get the call as we had heard plenty of wild tales about the region, and adventure seemed to have her hand out beckoning us to a mighty attractive possibility of new experience in a part of the USA that was pretty much untouched by the hand of what we considered as civilization."[3] For the first year in Gary, Beeson and Frank Boes, a long time friend from New York state, lived in a tent pitched by a stone quarry until company housing could be constructed.

While living in Gary, Beeson began exploring the mountains around the coal camp on hikes with Boes. Both he and Boes had heard of the famous Hatfield-McCoy feud, and visited the area

Beech Mountain - 1929
(Left to right) - Mary, Betty (aged five years old), Dick, Mrs. Elma Beeson, Ann, Mr.
D.R. Beeson. The family walked to the top of Beech Mountain from Banner Elk, North
Carolina.

in 1903. Beeson wrote that stories of the feud were in the news from California to Maine and "were no doubt, considerably magnified by the time they reached our very receptive ears." Beeson described meeting one of Hatfields in his account of this hike:

> A tall mountaineer appeared in the trail ahead, blocking our advance, so we pulled up for some talk. The stranger was a cadaverous looking guy but without the fierce, mean appearance we had been hoping to see. In fact he had a pleasant face tho the eyes were sharp and suspicious. He was dressed country fashion and carried a single-barrel shot gun. Our dreams of an ideal rough customer had faded . . . . It gave us a lift, of course, to learn that he was a Hatfield.[4]

Beeson remained at Gary for about two years, during which time he and Boes made several hikes into the mountains. At Gary, Beeson developed an interest in photography and began taking his camera with him on his walking trips.

In 1905, the construction of the company plants in Gary was completed, and Beeson moved to Bristol, on the Tennessee and Virginia border, to work for George L. Carter, who was building the Clinchfield Railroad. After a couple of years, Beeson moved to Johnson City, Tennessee, when Carter moved his office there. Eventually, the Clinchfield expanded into the Carolina, Clinchfield, and Ohio Railroad, which extended its line from Spartanburg, South Carolina through the mountains to Elkhorn City, Kentucky. Beeson's work with the Clinchfield took him through the mountainous regions of North Carolina, Tennessee, Virginia, and Kentucky. Beeson struck out on his own in 1912 when he opened his architectural practice in Johnson City.[5]

Dick, Betty and D. R. Beeson

Beeson's interest in hiking did not end in West Virginia. In Johnson City, Beeson found a new hiking companion in C. Hodge Mathes, professor of English and dean at the East Tennessee State Normal School. On their first adventure together, Beeson and Mathes spent a week in September 1913 on a walking trip from Roan Mountain, Tennessee, across Grandfather Mountain to Blowing Rock, North Carolina. The two men first traveled on the Carolina, Clinchfield and Ohio Railroad from Johnson City to Tocane, North Carolina, then by foot to Roan Mountain. Beeson documented each part of the journey with photographs, and both men kept daily diaries during the trip. In his diary entry for September 1, Beeson described the early morning walk to the Roan High Bluff and the view from the northwest face: "...the big mountains in the distance stick up thru the morning fogs like islands. I could look at such a sight for a month. . . . However, I suppose I would come to regard it differently in time, tho the beauty could never die, - only the novelty would wear off."[6] From the high bluff Beeson and Mathes traveled east to the High Knob near the Cloudland Hotel then followed the ridge at the Tennessee-North Carolina line to Grassy Ridge Bald, on toward Minneapolis, North Carolina and into Linville. On September 2, Beeson wrote they had gotten lost and it was his fault. He complained of passing through a grove of scrub beeches which was so thick they could not see out. They had to rely solely on the map and compass.[7]

On Grandfather Mountain Beeson and Mathes found parts of the trail almost impassable "where a step of a couple of feet to the side would land you at the base of the cliff some five hundred feet below." Near one of the three peaks of Grandfather Mountain, Beeson and Mathes met another party of four, two girls and a man with "an extra civilized look" and a native guide. Beeson commented that probably he and Mathes did not appear very civilized to them. The two men were

LeConte Lodge atop Mt. LeConte - 1928
(Left to right) - T.C. Fry, Mrs. Elma Beeson, Ann Beeson(in background), Louise Fry,
Dick Beeson, Caroline Beeson Fry (D.R. Beeson's sister) and D. R. Beeson. Both
families made the hike to Mt. LeConte by way of the Alum Cave Trail.

caught in a storm and were forced to spend the night in a cave on the mountain. Beeson noted that it was "worse to be on a mountain unable to get off than it is to be off when you can't get on."[8]

Beeson and Mathes spent the next two nights at Findley S. Gragg's farm near the eastern base of Grandfather Mountain, with a day trip over to Blowing Rock. Leaving the Gragg's home on September 6, Beeson and Mathes walked to Banner Elk, North Carolina, near Beech Mountain, and then went to Elk Park on the East Tennessee and Western North Carolina Railroad. The total walking distance of their trip was calculated to be 127 miles.[9]

Beeson and Mathes completed two walking trips through the mountains in 1914. On the first of the two hikes, Max Schoen and Buford Mathes accompanied them. The four men left Johnson City July 3 on the Carolina, Clinchfield, and Ohio Railroad and traveled through Erwin, Tennessee, and Spruce Pine, North Carolina, to the Linville Falls station. On the following day they began their hike along the Linville River to Table Rock and Hawksbill Mountains and back through the Linville River gorge to Linville Falls. Beeson commented that the "wildness of the region we are in makes the trip about the most satisfying I can imagine."[10]

The four hikers made camp near Linville Falls on the last night of their adventure. The walking trip ended the following day at an inn near Pineola, North Carolina, where they caught the train home to Johnson City.

The twosome of Beeson and Mathes ventured on a second trip in the late summer of the same year. This trek took them along the ridges of the Smoky Mountain range on the Tennessee-North Carolina state line. In an article for the Potomac Appalachian Trail Club Bulletin, Mathes blamed Horace Kephart for their "rash decision to tackle the Smoky skyline." Both men had read Kephart's book, Our Southern Highlanders, and were discussing it during the summer of 1914. Beeson recalled the part where at Hall's Cabin, Kephart turned back a man who was intent on continuing to Mount Guyot. Mathes agreed that Kephart probably saved the man's life and mentioned that Kephart cautioned it would be difficult for experienced woodsmen with a "party of axemen" to make the journey to Mount Guyot. Beeson replied that it sounded like a dare to him, and the two began planning the trip for the coming fall.[11]

On August 28, Beeson and Mathes took the Elkmont train from Knoxville to Riverside (now Kinzel Springs near Townsend) where they rode a lumber wagon for two and a half miles and walked another mile and a half to the home of Mathes' friend, W. H. Dunn, at the head of Dry Valley, Tennessee. The next day Beeson and Mathes walked south (18 miles in rain and fog) toward Thunderhead Mountain, near where they planned to spend the first night at a herdsmen's shelter known as the Spencer cabin.[12] Beeson and Mathes proceeded east along the ridge of the Smokies, roughly where the Appalachian Trail is now located.

The two men reached Mount Guyot on September 4 after a week long hike on low rations over difficult terrain. From the summit the two men descended 4,000 feet, often sliding on their stomachs to pass under the "laurel hells." They eventually reached a lumber camp at Big Creek where they were fed. They spent the last night in the company inn at Crestmont, North Carolina, and rode the train home the next morning. Beeson described this hike as the greatest of his walking trips and wondered where he would go next.[13]

The following year, Beeson and Mathes decided their next trip would be to the summit of Mount Mitchell. They began this journey on May 21 at Dolph Wilson's hotel in Murcheson, North Carolina. Beeson took pictures of the surrounding area, including a photograph of the old Tom Wilson cabin and of Dolph himself beside the skin of his 100th bear. Wilson agreed to guide the two men to the top of Mount Mitchell, and the three began the climb the following morning.[14]

Wilson took Beeson and Mathes to Mitchell Falls where his father, Tom, had discovered the body of Dr. Mitchell, the mountain's namesake. From the falls the men climbed a ravine which Beeson described as having the "same slope as a telegraph pole" and when they found a place flat enough, stopped for lunch. Of Wilson, Beeson noted that he had "seen men before who could walk up a steep mountain as fast as he can but have never known one before who could talk incessantly while doing it."[15]   They reached the summit of Mt. Mitchell at 2:00 pm, but since the weather prevented good visibility, the three men went to the government weather station on the mountain. Wilson returned home, and Beeson and Mathes descended the east side of the mountain along a lumber skidway. Beeson commented that the east side was "bare and burned over and not a pleasant sight at all."[16]

That evening Beeson and Mathes camped at the Blue Sea Fork of the Caney River which was just below the Pinnacle of the Blue Ridge. They hiked to the grassy knob of the Pinnacle the next morning. The two returned to Mt. Mitchell along a logging road. On May 24, they returned to Johnson City by way of the Carolina, Clinchfield, and Ohio Railroad.[17] The hike to the top of Mt. Mitchell was the last of Beeson and Mathes' extended walking trips into the mountains.

Beeson's interest in hiking and camping became lifelong following his early excursions with Mathes. A religious man, he became equally faithful to hiking and attempted to convert others to this pastime whenever the chance arose. His first attempt at a "conversion" concerned his wife, Elma Lillian Rankin Beeson. They met when Beeson, passing the open window of a church, heard her practicing a song.[18] Elma Rankin was a music teacher in the original faculty of East Tennessee

State Normal School (forerunner of East Tennessee State University) in Johnson City. The Beesons married in 1915, the year following the Great Smokies hike.

In August 1917, still early in their marriage, Don Beeson talked his wife into a week's hike in the Linville, North Carolina area. He called it a "co-ed" camping trip, and from the start it had some differences from his usual outings. As he noted in an unpublished account, "the eatables were a little above my usual grade and the gear included soap and towels for dishwashing,- a luxury peculiar to this one trip."[19] Mrs. Beeson wore "high shoes" laced up a few inches above the ankle, as was the custom for women then, according to Beeson. He himself wore his usual hiking attire-16-inch leather hiking boots, trousers, a light shirt and a necktie.[20]

The hike was remembered especially by Beeson (and his musical wife) for their visit with the McRae family, owners of Grandfather Mountain. The family was famous in the region for their bagpipe playing. "There were three of them at the time and they tuned up and gave us a short number as we paused on our way. It was some music; possibly it's a blessing that bagpipers are so scarce."[21]

The later part of the journey was also well remembered. They were forced to work their way to the railroad junction against pouring rain and flooded streams. Finally, they reached the Linville Falls station, "soaked to the skin." Mrs. Beeson had to be dried out behind the stove of a country store and was only half dried when they boarded the train for Johnson City. With dry understatement, Beeson notes that "it is the only co-ed camping trip of my experience."[22]

Beeson would later make a hike along this same line as escort to a party of industrialists from Kingsport who wanted to see some mountain scenery. He recalled the hard time he had getting the men (who were not in hiking shape) up to the mountain top. "At one time one of the men sat down on a rock and refused to go a step further, saying,- 'Here's where I get the effects of a Misspent life.'"[23] This might serve as the motto of many a well-meaning, ill-prepared hiker.

If the attempts to make hikers of his wife or the industrialists were not so successful, Beeson found more success with his children--D. R. "Dick" Beeson, Jr., Mary Beeson Ellison, Anna Beeson Gouge, and Betty Beeson Helms, whom he often took on outdoor excursions. Don Beeson also found long-term satisfaction in his involvement with the Boy Scouts of Johnson City Troop 8, sponsored by Calvary Presbyterian Church of which he was a member. Through these efforts he exposed another generation to the pleasures of hiking the wilderness.

In 1920 Beeson agreed to serve as temporary scoutmaster of Troop 8 until a permanent replacement could be found. The temporary appointment lasted for the next twenty years. Troop 8 gathered its membership from the "poorer" part of town. For Beeson it was an opportunity "for getting the boys in contact with religious and spiritual matters," a side of their natures which might otherwise have been equally "underprivileged."[24] A short devotional and prayer circle was a part of each scout meeting. Beeson also introduced twice a month hikes as a part of the regular routine. One was a day hike and one an overnight hike. In addition, a week long hiking/camping trip was held once a year. All this helped give the boys positive activities which kept them off the streets.

Over time Beeson developed a strong bond with his "boys." An architect by profession, he even designed and helped build a meeting house. Competition actually grew to gain admittance to the troop, as Beeson limited it to 32 boys at any one time. He was never easy on the troop, insisting that the boys earn anything they received. As would be noted in letters to him in latter life, such lessons served the scouts well in adulthood.

Troop 8
D. R. Beeson's boys.

The hikes were always vigorous, well planned, and often served to reinforce learning the boys received in school. One such hike was the attempt to locate the "Brown Mountain Lights" by survey triangulation. On this outing in the late 1920s, the troop divided into two groups, each with engineer's transits, one gang on Grandfather Mountain and one on Jonas Ridge. The groups sighted each other just before dark to get a baseline, with the idea of turning on the transit's lights after it got dark. It was a thoughtful plan, failing only to take into consideration the weather. "The night was unusually clear and none of us had ever seen the lights except when there was some haze in the air. So we came home next day without completing our triangle."[25]

Such excursions only increased the popularity of the troop and of hiking among the troopers. Beeson gave up active work as scoutmaster just before America's entry into World War II. However, he kept contact throughout the war with many of his former scouts who served in far flung outposts of the world. The conditioning of the hikes and the lessons on woodcraft and life learned under Beeson, no doubt, made all of them better soldiers when duty called.

Beeson had always taken an active interest in his scouts' lives, not just in that part which touched on scouting. As one of "Beeson's boys" would recall "he was well known at the junior and senior high schools because of his habit of visiting these schools to check on his boys' conduct and progress...He went even further with several of his boys and advanced them sufficient money for their college education...Today there are architects, engineers, draftsmen, contractors, and other business men who owe their success to [him]."[26]

Before, during, and after his scoutmaster career, Beeson remained an active hiker. As his architectural firm took more of his time, he had less time for extended hikes. A small hiking club was formed in 1930 around weekend hikes. It's members were Beeson, Hodge Mathes, Paul Fink

The A.B.F.M. Hiking Club
Paul Fink - Hodge Mathes - D.R. Beeson - Roy Ozmer
Cold Spring Mt. Spring 1925

(Jonesborough historian and naturalist), and local forest ranger Roy Ozmer (later known as "The Hermit of the Everglades"). They called their club "A. B. F. M. (Able bodied and Feeble minded)."[27] Even after this "club" folded under family and business responsibilities, Beeson continued fulfilling what must have been a "need" to hike, to be away from the press of the city whenever the chance allowed. He had the habit of leaving the office soon after lunch on Saturday, driving to the base of Buffalo Mountain (on the southern edge of Johnson City), and hiking to the summit (a distance of about two miles) and back. It was on such a hike in the late 1940s that Beeson's active hiking career came nearly to a disastrous end.

He had made it about a half mile along the trail when he passed "a slim, cadaverous mountaineer going the same direction and carrying a single barrel shotgun."[28] Beeson passed him and had gone on about 50 feet when he "heard a subdued crack from behind and felt a jar" on the back of his head. When "I felt the back of my head to investigate the damage, my hand came back covered with blood."[29] Unsure of how seriously he might be wounded, Beeson feared going back down the trail to his car, since he would have to pass the place where the shot had originated. However, his fear of bleeding to death overcame this latter fear, and he hurried back. "My hair stood up on end and my knees got weak and sweat ran down my back along with the blood...It didn't occur to me until afterwards that he had only one barrel to his gun." Beeson made it to the hospital safely, the wound actually being slight. The doctor removed four of seven shot, deciding "the other three ought to stay as a souvenir of the occasion,- they are still there."[30] Beeson's family, believing him to have encountered a moonshiner, refused him permission to hike Buffalo anymore. This did not deter him, however. He began driving some 10 miles further into Unicoi County to hike "the Pinnacle" there, and this remained his regular route for at least the next twenty years. In fact, he walked some six miles a day well into his eighties.

Beeson's love of hiking remained with him even after he could no longer actively engage in such extended journeys. He still made a determined effort to walk somewhere every day. Six years before his death in 1983, on his 96th birthday he wrote of his daily walk "to the Drug Store or Bank and back,"[31] a distance of about three blocks from the home he had designed years earlier, unaware that it would become base camp for this last "trail."

Norma Myers, Head of The Archives of Appalachia
Ned Irwin, Public Services Archivist

ENDNOTES

1. Beeson, D. R., Sr., "Autobiography," D.R. Beeson, Sr. Papers, Archives of Appalachia, East Tennessee State University, pp. 1-11.
2. Beeson, D. R., Sr., "Autobiography," pp. 2-11.
3. Reminiscences, D. R. Beeson, Sr. Papers, Archives of Appalachia, East Tennessee State University.
4. Reminiscences, D. R. Beeson, Sr. Papers, Archives of Appalachia, East Tennessee State University.
5. Beeson, D. R., Sr., "D. R. Beeson Itinerary-Uniontown to Johnson City," D. R. Beeson, Sr. Papers, Archives of Appalachia, East Tennessee State University.
6. Beeson, D. R., Sr., "Walking Trip, Grandfather Mountain," D. R. Beeson, Sr. Papers, p. 3.
7. Beeson, D. R., Sr., "Walking Trip, Grandfather Mountain," p. 5.
8. Beeson, D. R., Sr., "Walking Trip, Grandfather Mountain," pp. 9-13.
9. Beeson, D. R., Sr., "Walking Trip, Grandfather Mountain," pp. 19-20.
10. Beeson, D. R., Sr., "Walking Trip, Table Rock Mountain," D. R. Beeson, Sr. Papers, Archives of Appalachia, East Tennessee State University, pp. 1-4.

11. Mathes, Hodge. "A Week Among the Bears and Owls," <u>Potomac Appalachian Trail Club Bulletin</u> (July 1946) 65.

12. Mathes, "A Week among the Bears and Owls," p. 6; Beeson, D. R., Sr., "Walking Trip, Great Smoky Mountains," D. R. Beeson, Sr. Papers, Archives of Appalachia, East Tennessee State University, pp. 1-9.

13. Beeson, D. R., Sr., "Walking Trip, Great Smoky Mountains," pp. 29-33.

14. Beeson, D. R., Sr., "Walking Trip, Mt. Mitchell, N.C.," D. R. Beeson, Sr. Papers, Archives of Appalachia, East Tennessee State University, pp. 1-4.

15. Beeson, D. R., Sr., "Walking Trip, Mt. Mitchell," pp. 7-8.

16. Beeson, D. R., Sr., "Walking Trip, Mt. Mitchell," pp. 9-11.

17. Beeson, D. R., Sr., "Walking Trip, Mt. Mitchell," pp. 14-18.

18. D. R. Beeson, Sr. obituary, <u>Johnson City Press-Chronicle</u>, January 17, 1983, p. 2.

19. Beeson, D. R., Sr. "A Co-Ed Camping Trip, August 1917." D. R. Beeson, Sr. Papers, Archives of Appalachia, East Tennessee State University, p. 1.

20. Beeson, D. R., Sr., "A Co-Ed Camping Trip," p. 1.

21. Beeson, D. R., Sr., "A Co-Ed Camping Trip," p. 2.

22. Beeson, D. R., Sr., "A Co-Ed Camping Trip," p. 1.

23. Beeson, D. R., Sr., "A Co-Ed Camping Trip," p. 2-3.

24. Beeson, D. R., Sr. "Troop 8 History." D. R. Beeson, Sr. Papers, Archives of Appalachia, East Tennessee State University, p. 1.

25. Beeson, D. R., Sr., "Troop 8 History," p. 4.

26. Huff, Raymond E. letter, Feb. 4, 1971. D. R. Beeson, Sr. Papers, Archives of Appalachia, East Tennessee State University.

27. Beeson, D. R., Sr. letter, August 10, 1974. D. R. Beeson, Sr. Papers, Archives of Appalachia, East Tennessee State University.

28. Beeson, D. R., Sr. "Moonshining." D. R. Beeson, Sr. Papers, Archives of Appalachia, East Tennessee State University, p. 1.

29. Beeson, D. R., Sr., "Moonshining," p. 1.

30. Beeson, D. R., Sr., "Moonshining," p. 1.

31. Beeson, D. R., Sr. letter, May 3, 1977. D. R. Beeson, Sr. Papers, Archives of Appalachia, East Tennessee State University.

A Saga of the Carolina Hills
By C. Hodge Mathes

Nearly every schoolboy knows to-day that the highest mountain in the eastern part of the United States is Mount Mitchell, in North Carolina. A much smaller number, with a head for remembering figures, might possibly recall the altitude of that mountain-6,711 feet above the sea, though surprisingly few school geographies seem to record either of these two facts.

Far smaller still, I dare say, is the number of either children or grown-ups who have ever heard the story of how this crowning peak of eastern North America came to bear the name of Mitchell.

The chief actors in that story are two men: one a noted scholar and scientist, the other a gigantic hillsman, a mighty hunter of the bear and deer that for ages have roamed the fastnesses of the great Appalachian hinterland. It was from the lips of a son of this stalwart old hunter that I have heard, not once but often, many of the details of this true story that have never found their way into print. It has also been my good fortune to know at first hand and intimately the indescribably wild and remote region that furnishes the setting for the tale.

That region, to be sure, has now been discovered by the tourist, and a few of its outstanding points of interest may to-day be reached by motor. On my earliest visits, nearly a score of years ago, the only way to see Mount Mitchell or any of the vast wonderland of the Black Mountains was to go afoot, picking one's way through the eternal twilight of virgin forest along ancient trails that buffaloes, bears, and Indians had made long before a white man had ever glimpsed the Blue Ridge.

To begin the story properly we must go back nearly a decade before the Civil War. To most Americans at that time the great mountain masses of Tennessee and the Carolinas were a veritable terra incognita, sparsely populated by straggling descendants of the pioneers of the first transmontane migration, and inaccessible save by a

Summit of Mt. Mitchell, an engraving from <u>Harper's New Monthly Magazine</u>, November 1857, found in the North Carolina Museum of History, Raleigh; Reproduced by permission.

few steep and dangerous oxcart roads that sooner or later petered out among the highest hills into steeper and more dangerous bridle paths or game trails.

No official surveys of the Southern Appalachian had been undertaken by the government, and the altitude of the remote peaks of the Blue Ridge, the Unakas, and Great Smoky was unknown. Conflicting estimates, partly guesswork, partly based upon inaccurate private surveys and colored by local pride, were to be found in the fragmentary accounts that occasionally appeared in print.

A certain peak in Great Smoky, now known as Clingman's Dome (altitude 6,619 feet), was generally believed to be the highest point in the Appalachian system, and its height was often declared to be upward of 8,000 feet. Most New Englanders, on the other hand, stoutly maintained that Mount Washington in the White Mountains was the loftiest peak in the Eastern States.

About 1856 a committee in Congress was considering a request presented by certain citizens of North Carolina that the "Dome" of the Black Mountains, having been definitely ascertained to be the highest peak in the State, should be officially named

Rev. Elisha Mitchell (1793-1857).
The original is in the North
Carolina Museum of History,
Raleigh; Reproduced by
Permission.

D.C.Hinman.

Clingman's Peak, in honor of Hon. Thomas L. Clingman, of Buncombe County, who had served in the House of Commons and the Senate of the State and had been elected to Congress for a number of terms.

Before action had been taken upon this request the friends of Rev. Elisha Mitchell, professor of chemistry and geology in the State University at Chapel Hill, began to press the prior claims of this eminent and widely beloved scientist to receive the honor that was about to be bestowed upon the favorite political son.

Professor Mitchell was now about sixty-four years of age and had spent nearly forty years as an instructor in the University of his adopted State. A modest, retiring New England clergyman and geologist and mineralogist of note, he had endeared himself to all classes in the State. For years he had served as State surveyor and had spent many summers in the mountain sections on scientific explorations of various sorts.

The pupils, colleagues, and neighbors of Professor Mitchell now urged him, rather against his personal inclinations, to take steps to prove his claims as the real "discoverer" of the Black Dome, and a petition was prepared asking that the peak be given the name of Mitchell.

Toward the end of June, 1857, Professor Mitchell set out with a small party of friends to revisit the mountain which, twenty years before, he had first explored and had declared to be the highest peak in the system. It was his plan to look up some of the native guides and helpers who had accompanied him on that survey and secure their sworn statements to be filed with other documentary proofs with the Congressional committee.

It was a long and toilsome journey from Asheville to the balsam-crowned summit of the Dome, where he had years ago set a rough stone marker to indicate what he had calculated to be the highest point of land east of the Rockies. Having reached the top, however, Mitchell determined to dismiss his companions and to continue his journey, afoot and alone, down into the deep valley on the Yancey side of the great ridge, where he wished to secure an affidavit from an old trapper and guide by the name of Green. He knew he could count on the help and the hospitality of the loyal mountaineers who had come to know and love the "Perfesser" in years gone by.

That parting with his friends at the top of the Black Dome was the last time Elisha Mitchell was ever seen alive. When he had not returned on the third day his family became alarmed. Next day a small searching party set out to find him. It was soon learned that he had never reached the home of his old guide, and none of the mountain folk had seen or heard of him.

A general alarm was now given, and a large party, headed by the popular statesman, Zebulon Baird Vance, began a day-and-night manhunt, combing one after another of the interminable ridges and ravines with dogs and lanterns and keeping in touch with each other by prearranged gunshot signals. Several days passed, however, without a single trace of the lost man.   The whole State was aroused, from the cities of the Coastal Plain to the scattered settlements of the western mountains.

On the tenth or eleventh day the distressing news had penetrated to a sequestered cove on the farther side of the Blacks. Here a small party was organized by one of the most romantic characters that ever lived in the Carolina hills, "Big Tom" Wilson, gigantic of frame, a stranger to fear, and familiar with every mile of the dark wilderness of the Black Mountains. Big Tom possessed in a remarkable degree that almost uncanny power that few save the Indians have ever acquired, of reading the "signs" of man or beast in the woods.

The veteran hunter led his party of seasoned mountain men to the top of the Dome and securing from the watchers there the meager details of Mitchell's last conversation with his Asheville friends, took up the search by a plan all his own.

Learning that the Professor had declared his intention of following the old "Beech Nursery" trail to the foot of the mountain, Big Tom and his party set out in single file, the sinewy giant in the lead. He had gone scarcely half a mile when his practiced eye caught something significant that all the other parties had missed.

"Look, boys!" he exclaimed. "Right here's whar the ol' man missed the trail! Instid of bearin' on to the left, like he ought, he turned off down t'wards the Piny Ridge. An' right that minute he was lost, an' bad lost!"

Sure enough, as they pressed on down the right-hand trail, which was probably only a bear path, here and there appeared the faint but still recognizable tracks of a man, headed toward the desolate waste under the frowning tops of the twin peaks known as the "Black Brothers."

"He couldn't have been makin' no time in here, boys," Big Tom declared half an hour later as the going grew worse and more dangerous. "See how he's had to tromp down the bresh an' scrouge through the laurel! An' here's a piece tore out of his coat!"

Two miles or more they pushed on—slow, wearisome miles even for the sturdy mountaineers. For the aged scientist, long unpracticed in such tramping, it must have been a grilling experience.

Thomas D. (Big Tom) Wilson (1823-1908) led the search party that found Rev. Mitchell's body in 1857. Big Tom is the father of Dolph Wilson who led Beeson and Mathes. The original photo is in the North Carolina Museum of History, Raleigh; Reproduced by Permission.

TOM WILSON.

Engraving of Big Tom Wilson. The North Carolina Museum of History, Raleigh; Reproduced by Permission.

"Here's whar dark overtuck him," the guide announced after another mile had been covered. "Look whar he twisted him a pine knot out o' this ol' log an' made him a torch! Here's a coal that drapped when he crossed this rock!"

Two more miles, through tangled briars, over jagged ledges, and down the boulder-strewn bed of a little creek.

"'Course by this time he knowed he was lost," the leader commented, "but he figgered that this here creek would take him to the Cane River, which naturally hit would, only hit's a turrible way to git thar!"

A few hundred yards more and the roar grew louder. They were on the very top of the ledge.

"Look, boys!" Big Tom sang out. "He was tryin' to git around on the right of this place in the nighttime! See, he grabbed holt of this little saplin' an' his foot slipped on this slick rock. The saplin' broke off in his hand! Boys, that pore ol' man has fell right over them falls! We'll find him down thar as shore as the world!"

Clambering down over the rocks and through the undergrowth, the party at last reached the foot of the cliff, over which tumbled a foaming cascade approximately twenty feet high. At its foot was a dark, deep, jug-shaped pool of swirling foam ten or twelve feet across. Even the strongest swimmer could not have kept afloat in that mad little whirlpool.

At first they could see nothing in the churning water, but finally Big Tom made out a dark object underneath the surface lying across a sunken birch log that had long ago fallen into the pool. And in the gloom of that sunless gorge they lifted the body of Elisha Mitchell from its watery tomb.

Sadly and with prodigious labor they bore their burden back up the long miles and delivered it to the friends waiting at the top. Big Tom and the other mountaineers urged that it be laid to rest there on the spot that his travels and explorations had made memorable, but other counsels prevailed, and the body was carried back to Asheville and buried in the Presbyterian cemetery.

Years afterwards, however, when government surveys had confirmed Mitchell's calculations and the Black Dome, officially and finally named in his honor, had become one of the chief points of scenic and historic interest in the State, the bones were exhumed and carried back to be deposited in a rocky grave at the very summit of the peak.

A modest shaft of hollow bronze bearing a simple inscription was erected by relatives and friends at the grave, but the fierce storms that sweep the summit finally wrecked it. Then a wooden observation tower, built by the State Park Commission, took its place. This was later replaced by a steel tower, but it also fell before the fury of the winds. Very recently a beautiful and massive tower of stone, the gift of a public-spirited citizen of the State, has been reared on the site of the grave. Its top, rising above the low timber, affords one of the most impressive panoramas to be found on the American continent.

Of late Mount Mitchell has come into its own as a goal for the throngs of those who go "seeing America first." It is one of the show places of the South. Two excellent motor roads have been built to the top, and thousands of tourists make the ascent each season.

Frankly, though, this mountaineering de luxe does not give much of a thrill to those of us who used to camp under the big "rock-house" just below the top, or in the old log cabin that later stood there. Dearer to us were those never-to-be-forgotten nights under the stars, where the cool wind in the balsams and the occasional scream of a wild cat or a mountain owl gave us a weird sense of solitariness, knowing we were the only human beings in the vast loneliness of the Black Mountains.

Big Tom Wilson lived more that fifty years after what he always called his greatest adventure, the finding of Mitchell's body.   He was the greatest hunter and trapper in all the mountain settlements. One hundred and fourteen black bears fell to his rifle, a record as yet unsurpassed, as far as I have authentic information, in the Southern Appalachians.

Honest to the core, kind of heart, keenly intelligent although unlettered, devoutly religious, and thrifty as only a canny Scotch-Irish hillsman knows how to be, he left a goodly estate of mountain lands, a worthy family of sons and daughters, and a name that is yet honored in his native hills. In the sequestered world in which he lived his eighty-five years he reigned as one of nature's own princes. Quite fittingly the beautiful valley where his cabin home stood and still stands is marked on the topographic maps of the Geological Survey as "Big Tom Wilson's".

His sons and his sons' sons have preserved the estate and cherished the traditions of their doughty progenitor. It was one of these sons, Dolph Wilson, himself now nearing seventy, who gave me much of the story I have recorded here. With him I have tramped the obscure trail over which his father piloted the searchers for Mitchell's body. Only with such a guide could one ever hope to find the desolate "Mitchell's Falls," a spot that few visitors have ever seen.

Dolph is himself a veteran nimrod and has killed a total of a hundred and eleven bears. It is characteristic of the man that he has now quit the chase for good, not because of his age but in order that his father's famous record shall continue unbroken in the traditions of the bear country.

Dolph has prospered far beyond the average of mountain folk and is reputed wealthy in the hills. He is a local magistrate and his "court" is wholesomely feared by the petty lawbreaker.

Fortunate is the party of tourists who can nowadays have Dolph Wilson as a guide. He is a bush man, for despite his sixty-eight years he patrols almost daily an extensive boundary that he has leased as a game preserve to a hunting and fishing camp in Asheville, and he can still walk the legs off a tenderfoot.

Dolph Wilson represents the finest traditions of the sturdy pioneers. He loves to sit on his porch in the starlight and tell of the early days—the old rifles, the old trails, the old customs. But he looks the modern world level in the face with an eye as cool as that which used to gaze down the sights of his trusty Winchester at a wounded and charging bear.

In 1888, thirty-one years after Elisha Mitchell's death, a monument was erected on the summit of Mt. Mitchell over Mitchell's grave. The monument was destroyed in early 1915 just months before Beeson and Mathes went on their hike. *North Carolina Collection, Pack Memorial Public Library, Asheville, North Carolina. Reproduced by Permission.*

C. Hodge Mathes
(1879-1951)

Charles Hodge Mathes was an educator in the highest sense of the word, who his life in learning and teaching. His academic credentials included: an A.B. from Washington College in 1897, a Masters from Maryville College in 1904, further work at the University of Wooster, Harvard, McGill University, and Middlebury College.

Teaching was what Hodge Mathes lived. He served as a professor at Washington College (1897-1903), Maryville College (1903-1911), East Tennessee State University (1911-1949), and Milligan College (1949-1951). In his career he taught Greek, English, Modern Languages, and Education. At one time he served East Tennessee State College (now East Tennessee State University) as dean, registrar, professor of English, professor of Education and chairman of the foreign language department.

His career in education was not without its rough spots. Ever popular with students, he sometimes ran afoul of others. Once when Dean Hodge Mathes' salary had been raised from $2,100 to $2,400, the East Tennessee Democratic leader, Thad A. Cox complained to Governor Tom C. Rye. Cox's main objection was that Mathes was a staunch Republican.

In 1925, Hodge Mathes was nominated for the presidency of East Tennessee State Teachers College. However, Charles C. Sherrod was selected as the second president of the college. Mathes worked closely with Sherrod until both retired in 1949. Hodge Mathes did not retire voluntarily but did so only because he had reached the state mandatory retirement age of seventy. He left East Tennessee State University to teach the last two years of his life at nearby Milligan College.

Hodge Mathes believed strongly in the work he was doing at the state teachers college in Johnson City. He said that Tennessee needed "trained thinkers, professional leaders, and public servants with a broad vision, wide culture, and courageous character," and that the "training of such leaders demanded the soundest scholarship and most vigorous discipline in every field of learning." Mathes applied these words to his own life with studies in such diverse fields as archeology, architecture and history.

He wrote several books and numerous short stories which were published in several magazines. A collection of his stories was recently published under the title In The Shadow of Old Smoky. Composition and Grammar was published in 1919. With Frank Field, a fellow professor at East Tennessee State, he authored Safety in the Danger Age and Book I in the Safety Education Series. However his best work was in fiction about the mountains and their people.

When the Normal School and East Tennessee State Teachers College were set up in Johnson City in 1911, Hodge Mathes was the second person hired. Notes from freshmen of 1911 in the Normal School were sent to Mrs. Wynema Souder Mathes at Hodge Mathes' death. These letters of condolence express some of the character of their beloved teacher:

"Among all the teachers I had in high school, college and university days, Professor Mathes was my favorite, the one who awakened me and gave me most. He it was who made the English

The Normal School Faculty (1912) - C. Hodge Mathes is the first person on the left end of the second row. Lillian Rankin, who later became D. R. Beeson's wife, is the third from the right on the first row. President Sidney G. Gilbreath is fourth from the left on the back row.

language a fascinating, challenging world of exquisite beauty for my exploration; who intrigued me to dare explorations in the Anglo-Saxon, the Greek, and other cultures. He imparted to me his own love of mountain climbing, and in my far travels I have remembered him particularly when struggling up some peak of the Alps or other great mountain face. He stimulated me in ways that created hungers and thirsts in my spirit for a richer life. I am deeply indebted and always will be indebted to him for his teaching and his influences upon me when I was a teen-ager." (W. Earl Hotalen)

"Professor Mathes was one of the first teachers I met and he was assigned to teach our English Class. The first day our class met I felt I was going to enjoy this subject for Professor Mathes seemed to be so thorough and patient. This did prove to be a very interesting class and I learned something each day from his instructions. Professor Mathes had a very brilliant mind, a wonderful personality and was so kind and generous to all. I shall, indeed, remember him as a great person." (Agnes E. Dyer)

"Because he never lost his own zest for acquiring new knowledge, he was able to impart much of his own enthusiasm to his students. His search for the exact word; the finish he gave even to his informal talks; the little gesture of the head by which he emphasized a point; these all stand out in memory." (Gertrude Williams Miller)

"When we were young, with ideas shooting in all directions, and growing too fast for our clothes, we found a friend who stayed with us forty years.

President Sidney Gilbreath and C. Hodge Mathes in a wagon in front of the Normal School in 1912.

"He smiled at us with a kindliness that steadied our nerves and made our voices more gentle, although he did seem to enjoy the bouncing vitality of that first-year class. He knew our names and natures, and how to help us through the pitfalls of adolescence. With his quick insight and obviously high cultural standards, he led us gently into a brighter world, teaching us that sympathetic understanding makes every life happier." (The First-Year Pupils in the High School, 1911, East Tennessee State Normal)

Mathes kept in touch with his students. He followed them throughout their careers. He, along with Dean David Sinclair Burelson, started the alumni association at East Tennessee State College in 1925. Later, in the fall of 1935, Eleanor Carlock and Mathes began publishing the Alumni Quarterly.

Hodge Mathes was no stranger to the mountains about which he wrote so eloquently. He was born in Maryville, Tennessee, to a Presbyterian minister and his wife on April 3, 1879. The first six years of his life, young Hodge grew up in the shadow of the Smokies while his father served a Presbyterian church in Maryville. In 1885, the family moved to Washington College in Upper East Tennessee where his father taught Greek and Latin.

When Hodge completed his first degree at Washington College he began teaching at his alma mater. In 1902 he married Wynema Souder of Indiana. They moved to Maryville in 1903 where Mathes taught Greek, Latin, and the Romance languages. The Matheses had two children, Ralph and Mildred.

The love of the mountains of East Tennessee and Western North Carolina was not just an academic or literary interest. Hodge Mathes loved to be out in the mountains, walking and climbing. In 1913, 1914, and 1915, he shared four adventurous hikes with his friend, D.R. Beeson,Sr., a Johnson City architect.

The first of these trips was a walking tour over Roan and Grandfather Mountains from August 31 to September 7, 1913. Beeson recorded their adventures in a hike journal which is illustrated with photographs taken on the trek. In 1914 they traveled to Table Rock Mountain in North Carolina from July 3 to the 6th.

Their next journey was only a few weeks later when they went by train to Kinzel Springs near Townsend, Tennessee. They walked into the Smokies from the train station to traverse the crest line of the Smokies from Spence Field to Mount Guyot. In the absence of marked trails, they often were lost. This hike roughly followed the route on which the Appalachian Trail would be blazed nearly twenty year later. They walked from August 28 to September 4. When they reached the lumber camp at Crestmont they were hungry because they had run out of food.

On their travels, they met many people who lived and worked in the area. Beeson joked that Hodge Mathes seemed to have mutual acquaintances with nearly all the mountaineers. Mathes made friends among the people of the mountains. His stories reflect these friendships.

The fourth journey was to Mt. Mitchell in May of 1915. On this trip they met Dolph Wilson, the son of Big Tom Wilson--the hero of "A Saga of the Carolina Hills." It was on this trip that they heard the story that Mathes recorded in that story.

Hodge Mathes made many other hiking trips into the mountains. The walks with Beeson were well documented with text and pictures. Mathes drew on these walking experiences as he wrote his own fictional accounts of life in the mountains. His familiarity with the geography of the region is evident from his writings. Often the actual names of places and geographical points were fictionalized. However, those that are familiar with the terrain of East Tennessee and Western North Carolina are never lost in Hodge Mathes' stories.

In addition to his love of the mountains, Hodge Mathes had a love of languages. His ear for languages and dialects is well recorded in his stories. He was a "linkster" who could listen to and reproduce everyday talk. This was a day before tape recorders. His memory for languages must have been excellent. The fact that he was proficient in several languages (Greek, Latin, German, French, Italian, and Russian) is evidence enough.

The stories that Mathes wrote show his own use of English. His command of the language is beautiful. He records the dialect of the mountain people with accuracy and respect. Reading the mountain dialect can be difficult. Sometimes it is best to read it aloud so that the sound of the words can be heard. Mathes enjoyed the mountain speech because it sometimes preserved Elizabethean English.

In general, Hodge Mathes simply loved the people of the mountains. Whenever he listened to the mountain talk of his highland neighbors it was with a sympathetic ear. His writings reflect the sheer joy of this man who reveled in the mountains and their people.

GLOSSARY

Black Mountain Country: A range of North Carolina mountains, including Mt. Mitchell, extending from the Buncombe-Yancey County line northeast to south central Yancey County.

Blue Sea Falls: Located on Blue Sea Creek in southern Yancey County, North Carolina, and is today within the Pisgah National Forest.

Brown Brothers camp: A local lumber company. No other information has been found.

C. C. & O.: Carolina, Clinchfield & Ohio Railroad. The Archives and Special Collections division of the Sherrod Library, East Tennessee State University, Johnson City has the existing company records.

Caney River: Also known as Cane River, rises in the Black Mountains of Yancey County, North Carolina and joins the Toe River on the Yancey-Mitchell County line to form the Nolichucky River, which flows into Tennessee.

Clingman, T. L.: Thomas L. Clingman (1812-1897), a soldier, U. S. Congressman and Senator from North Carolina, was a member of the first party to measure what was later named Clingmans Dome on the border between North Carolina and Tennessee in the present-day Great Smoky Mountains National Park.

Deacon: Beeson's nickname for C. Hodge Mathes.

Dub: A clumsy, unskilled person.

Grandfather Mountain: Located at the junction of Avery, Caldwell, and Watauga Counties in North Carolina, the mountain is today a privately owned tourist attraction.

<u>Great Craggy Mountains</u>: A range south west of Mt. Mitchell which includes Craggy Dome.

<u>The Hawksbill</u>: Point on Jonas Ridge near Table Rock Mountain in Burke County, North Carolina. Beeson and Mathes had hiked here in 1914.

<u>Johnson City, Tennessee</u>: Located in Washington County in upper East Tennessee, this was home to both Beeson and Mathes and is approximately 45 miles north east of the Mt. Mitchell area.

<u>Laurel</u>: Beeson's referral to laurel probably is a reference to rhododendron.

<u>Dr. Mitchell</u>: Rev. Elisha Mitchell (1793-1857), professor at the University of North Carolina, fell to his death in June of 1857 while attempting to prove that the mountain later to be named after him was indeed the highest point east of the Mississippi River.

<u>Mitchell Falls</u>: Site where Dr. Mitchell fell to his death on Mt. Mitchell. The waterfall is forty feet high, with a fifteen foot deep pool at its base.

<u>Murcheson, North Carolina</u>: A community on the Cane River in southern Yancey County.

<u>Normal School</u>: East Tennessee State Normal School in Johnson City, Tennessee, which opened in 1911 and which is today known as East Tennessee State University. Mathes was at the time of this hike serving as dean of the school.

<u>Pearley & Crockett Lumber Co.</u>: Founded by Fred A. Perley and W.H. Crockett, prominent lumbermen from Williamsport, Pennsylvania, the company bought the timber rights to 9,000 acres on Mt. Mitchell in 1913 and logged the site until 1921.

<u>Pensacola, North Carolina</u>: Community on Cane River in southern Yancey County, named from the Indian word meaning "hair people," for those who wore their hair long.

<u>The Pinnacle</u>: A peak located southwest of Mt. Mitchell where the counties of Buncombe, McDowell, and Yancey meet.

<u>Niagara Falls Riddle</u>: Granddaughter of Big Tom Wilson.

<u>Rattlesnake "nannygoat"</u>: A popular antidote used with a hypodermic needle. Nannygoat is Beeson's word play on "antidote." Horace Kephart in his 1917 Camping and Woodcraft writes: "The only positive antidote for snake poison, after it has entered the circulation, is anti-venom serum. This is prepared by injecting into a horse or mule a factional dose of the venom of a snake, or a mixture of those different species. When the animal recovers from the effects of this preliminary doese, a slightly larger one is injected and so on, every two or three weeks, for a year or two. Finally the serum of the animal's blood has developed an anti-toxin that makes him immune to snake venom. Some of this blood is then withdrawn, and the serum is separated, sterilized, and put up either in liquid or dried form in sealed tubes. These must be kept in a cool, dark place, to preserve the serum from deteriorating. A large hypodermic syringe is used to inject the serum into a patient. This treatment will cure the gravest cases of snake bite, if employed before the victim has collapsed. As it is not toxic, it is safe for even inexperienced people to use." (Horace Kephart, <u>Camping and Woodcraft</u>. Knoxville: University of Tennessee Press, 1988)

<u>Rubbering</u>: A term for those who turn to look at something or an event. "Rubber necking" is the more common term.

<u>The Smokies</u>: Great Smoky Mountains on the border of Tennessee and North Carolina where Beeson and Mathes had hiked the year before. Today the route of the hike is located within the Great Smoky Mountains

National Park. Beeson's account of the hike, *In The Spirit of Adventure A 1914 Smoky Mountain Hiking Journal*, has been published by Panther Press.

Table Rock: Table Rock Mountain in northwest Burke County, North Carolina, is today located within the Pisgah National Forest. Beeson and Mathes had hiked here in 1914.

Toe River Gap: The Toe River in North Carolina is formed on the Mitchell-Yancey County line near Boonford and flows northwest to its junction with Cane River, then forming the Nolichucky River, which flows on into Tennessee. The Gap itself is located between the Pinnacle and Bald Knob to the southwest of Mt. Mitchell.

Dolph Wilson: Son of Big Tom Wilson, noted hunter, and Beeson and Mathes' guide on the Mt. Mitchell hike.

Big Tom Wilson: (1823-1908) Noted hunter and guide whose home stood near Mt. Mitchell. It was Wilson who in 1857 found the body of Rev. Elisha Mitchell following his fatal fall on the mountain later named after him.

Yeates Knob: A mountain known today as Big Butte located on the Buncombe-Yancey County line southwest of Flat Springs Gap. It has also been known as Wilson Knob.

ACKNOWLEDGEMENTS

The assitance of D. R. Beeson' family is gratefully acknowledged. D. R. (Dick) Beeson, Jr. of Johnson City, Tennessee, Mary Rankin Beeson Ellison of Winter Park, Florida, Ann Campbell Beeson Gouge of Johnson City, Tennessee, and Elma Elizabeth (Betty) Beeson Helms of Neenah, Wisconsin assisted through their memories of hikes with their father and mother as well as with cherished family photographs which they generously shared.

Also, thanks to Georgia Greer of The Archives of Appalachia, who transcribed the original journal and to Jean Speer, the Director of the Center for Appalachian Studies and Services for her support. East Tennessee State University is appreciated for its role in providing personnel and support in the valuable area of preserving and protecting Appalachian history.

The work at Panther Press could not take place without the diligent service and careful eyes of David and Lin Morris, Hal and Elizabeth Hubbs, and Janice Maynard. Their foresight in bringing this series of journals to the light of publication is truly appreciated.

In The Spirit of Adventure Series

A 1913 Roan and Grandfather Mountains Hiking Journal

A 1914 Table Rock Mountain Hiking Journal

A 1914 Smoky Mountain Hiking Journal

A 1915 Mount Mitchell Hiking Journal

The books are $12.95 for hardback versions and $7.95 for paperback.

Also available from Panther Press are C. Hodge Mathes' stories of mountain life under the title <u>In The Shadow of Old Smoky</u>. Hardback editions are $12.95 and paperbacks are $8.95. A one hour audio tape of four of Mathes' stories as told by storyteller Charles Maynard, who edited the Beeson and Mathes books, is available for $8.95.

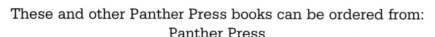

These and other Panther Press books can be ordered from:
Panther Press
P.O. Box 636 Seymour, Tennessee 37865
Telephone: 423-573-5792   Fax Number: 423-573-5697